CHRISTMAS

Dedicated to the Christ in Christmas!

Author: Caryn E. Southerland
Illustrator: Jacob J. Beagley

'Twas the night before Christmas
when all through our home,
Everybody was quiet
and the dogs did not roam.

The stockings were hung
by the chimney with care
In hopes that St. Nicholas
soon would be there.

The kids were asleep -
just beginning to snore.
Christmas in the Ozarks
had arrived once more.

I, in my pj's,
and Mom close to sleeping;
TV was on,
but I was not peeping!

A noise from outside
arose in the night.
It was so loud
I awoke with a fright.

Off the couch I sprang,
and to the window I flew.
Rubbing my peepers
to examine the view.

When what to my wondering
eyes should appear?
It should be St. Nick! -
But those aren't reindeer!

The moon o'er the Ozarks
made it easy to see.
My mind was puzzled,
"How could this be?"

As the sleigh flew over
in the dense, winter fog
It was clear that this carriage
was pulled by some hogs!

There was a fat little driver
so plump and so red.
Hum-m-m-m, something is different,
I thought in my head.

He snorted his orders
to the six little pigs
As they squealed and
galloped to land this rig.

The sleigh came to rest
on our yard in the dark.
"Whoa, Pork Chop!" "Whoa, Ham Bone!"
I heard him bark.

From his tusks to his snout,
to his hooves that clicked.
I knew this was not
the familiar St. Nick.

He was chubby and plump
and his nose you would note.
His curly, little tail
stuck out of his coat!

He jumped out of the sleigh
and trudged through the yard.
When he came to the door,
he knocked very hard.

Though I did not answer,
he came right on in.
Toting his bag,
tucked under his chin.

His eyes, they twinkled!
His snout, how merry!
Ears were quite pointed.
His cheeks were like cherries!

He had curly white tusks
that sparkled in the light.
And the ridge down his back
looked as sharp as a knife.

He paused for a moment,
when inside the door,
Then strode straight away,
across the floor.

Right to the tree,
with his sack in his hand,
To distribute the gifts,
according to plan.

All of sudden
he stopped in his tracks.
His eyes glazed over;
he put down his pack.

It was cookies and milk
that made him stop.
Treats for "Santa".
He was smacking his chops!

He snorted and rooted,
he just could not wait!
He drank and he gobbled -
even the plate!

With a satisfied grunt,
he unloaded his sack.
He had presents for all.
No one would lack!

Now, time to trot;
he made his way out.
And I got a good look
at the size of that snout!

He jumped in his sleigh
and drove out of sight.

I heard,

"SOO, PIG

SOOOOOIE

And to all a good night!!"

Meet the Characters:

Rayz

Ham Bone

Pigman

Pork Chop

Bacon

Boar-us

Root-y

Peaty

(My name is Peaty because I like to repeat what I see!)
I especially like to play hide and seek.

Turn the page to see if you can find me as I have hidden
myself in familiar scenes of the Ozarks.
If you can find me 14 times, you are a genius!

About the Author

Hello, I'm Caryn Southerland! Born, raised, educated, and totally blessed right here in the Ozarks! I love my family and I love the fact that my family loves to laugh. My mom and grandmother would often write entertaining poems to celebrate special occasions. Their words would take on familiar rhythms to humorously express the moment: who we were, where we lived, and much of what we lived through! The objective was to shift our sober, sometimes much too serious attitude to a little lighter one; one in which we could laugh, even enjoy our age or stage of life!

My greatest desire for you is that you could read (hopefully out loud) and laugh and then, share both with a child – of any and all ages! Making a "together" memory around the holidays is a lasting treasure.

About the Illustrator

Jacob Beagley is my name. I am a 2013 high school graduate and completer of my first year of college. Recently, I decided to continue my education while also serving in the United States Army. I am looking forward to supporting our country and taking the opportunity to learn many new skills. To add to all this excitement and change, I have also recently married! My drawings are a gift to me and I hope, for others. They are my retreat as much as they are my expression. It is my hope that I can bring you a smile and chuckle through these images of a jolly pig and a funny little mouse, I call Peaty!

About the Graphic Designer

Leia Morshedi here! First, thank you for reading Ozark Christmas. Now, a little about me – I was born and raised in Central Arkansas and received a Bachelor of Arts in Communication from the University of Central Arkansas in 2003. In 2005 I moved to Chicago where I worked with many talented and truly awesome people before moving back home to be with my family in 2011. I have over seven years of marketing/advertising focused graphic design experience that stretches across all mediums. My passion lies in brand consistency and in strategic problem-solving, which goes far beyond the art board.

Follow us on Facebook: facebook.com/ozarkchristmas

Web: ozarkchristmas.com